HISTORY & GEOGRAPHY 502
A NEW NATION

Author:
Theresa Buskey, J.D.

Editor:
Alan Christopherson, M.S.

Illustrations:
Brian Ring

Media Credits:
Page 3: © Gina Groves, iStock, Thinkstock **5:** © Alice Scully, iStock, Thinkstock; **8:** © Comstock, Stockbyte, Thinkstock; **11:** © Paula Stephens, iStock, Thinkstock; **12:** © Christine Reyes, iStock, Thinkstock; **14, 38, 43:** © Steven Wynn, iStock, Thinkstock; **15, 26, 41, 47:** © Photos.com, Thinkstock; **20:** © Sascha Burkard, Hemera, Thinkstock; **22:** © Jupiterimages, LiquidLibrary,Thinkstock; **28:** © Mark Tenniswod, iStock, Thinkstock; **30:** © Wessam Eldeeb, iStock, Thinkstock; **31:** © lucky spark, iStock, Thinkstock; **36:** © robeo, iStock, Thinkstock; **40:** © Chalky-White, iStock, Thinkstock; **44:** © stocksnapper, iStock, Thinkstock; **46:** © Thinkstock Images, Stockbyte, Thinkstock.

All maps in this book © Map Resources, unless otherwise stated.

Alpha Omega
PUBLICATIONS

804 N. 2nd Ave. E.
Rock Rapids, IA 51246-1759

A NEW NATION

The United States of America was born on July 4, 1776, the day the Declaration of Independence was accepted by Congress. The nation was not really free, however, until after the War for Independence was fought. Americans fought for their freedom for eight long, hard years. They might have given up many times, but they did not. Britain finally granted the United States its independence in 1783 after losing two armies in America.

The war was only the beginning. After it was over, the new nation had to write a constitution that would work. It also had to start up a new government that was not like any other in the world! George Washington, who had led the American army to victory, was chosen as the nation's first president. He started the nation off right by his fairness and firmness in those first years. By God's grace, the nation was born and survived its first years.

Objectives

Read these objectives. The objectives tell you what you will be able to do when you have successfully completed this LIFEPAC®. Each section will list according to the numbers below what objectives will be met in that section. When you have finished this LIFEPAC, you should be able to:

1. Name the major battles and leaders in the Revolutionary War.
2. Describe the government under the Articles of Confederation.
3. Describe the decisions made at the Constitutional Convention and the government created by the Constitution.
4. Explain how the Constitution became the government of America.
5. Describe the problems and actions of the first president of the United States.
6. Describe life in the United States when the new government began.
7. Describe the beginning of political parties and important events under the second president of the United States.

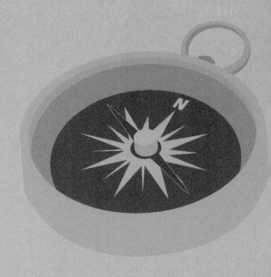

1. WAR FOR INDEPENDENCE

The Revolutionary War lasted from 1775 to 1783. It began at Lexington in Massachusetts and ended at Yorktown in Virginia. It was fought all over the colonies.

The British should have won easily. They were a powerful nation with a large army and navy. The United States was a very weak country with a small army that was made up of men from the militia. However, God had His own plans. The British fought very poorly, and the Americans would not give up.

Finally, the French decided to help the Americans. They wanted revenge for the loss of New France. With French help, the Americans trapped and defeated a whole British army. Then, Britain agreed to end the war and give America its independence.

Objectives

Review this objective. When you have completed this section, you should be able to:

1.   Name the major battles and leaders in the Revolutionary War.

Vocabulary

Study these new words. Learning the meanings of these words is a good study habit and will improve your understanding of this LIFEPAC.

ally (al' ī). A nation united with another for some special purpose.

betray (bi trā). To be unfaithful or disloyal to.

cannon (kan' ən). A big gun supported by wheels or a flat base.

colonel (kėr' nl). Officer ranking above a major and below a general.

promote (prə mōt). To raise in rank or importance.

siege (sēj). The surrounding of a fortified place by an army trying to capture it.

spokesman (spōks' mən). A person who speaks for another or others.

spy (spī). A person who tries to get information about the enemy, usually in time of war, by visiting the enemy's territory in disguise.

traitor (trā' tər). A person who betrays his or her country.

Note: *All vocabulary words in this LIFEPAC appear in* **boldface** *print the first time they are used. If you are unsure of the meaning when you are reading, study the definitions given.*

Pronunciation Key: h**a**t, **ā**ge, c**ã**re, f**ä**r; l**e**t, **ē**qual, t**ė**rm; **i**t, **ī**ce; h**o**t, **ō**pen, **ô**rder; **oi**l; **ou**t; c**u**p, p**u̇**t, r**ü**le; **ch**ild; lo**ng**; **th**in; /₮H/ for **th**en; /zh/ for mea**s**ure; /u/ or /ə/ represents /a/ in **a**bout, /e/ in tak**e**n, /i/ in penc**i**l, /o/ in lem**o**n, and /u/ in circ**u**s.

A Bleak Beginning

Problems. The Revolutionary War was not a fair fight. The British had many advantages. Britain was one of the most powerful nations on earth in 1775. It had a large army and navy. It had money to hire soldiers from Germany (Hessians). Also, many Americans still did not want independence. They were loyal to the king. These people, called *Tories*, would help the British against the patriots.

Another problem was the American government. The Second Continental Congress took over as a government for all the colonies in 1776, but it had no power. It could not collect taxes, only the state assemblies could do that.(The original thirteen colonies had all become states.) Congress could only ask for money, and they often did not get it. That made it very difficult to pay the soldiers and buy supplies for them. Britain did not have that problem. Its soldiers were better paid and supplied all through the war.

However, the British had some problems too. Their generals were usually noblemen who had paid for their place in the army. Many of them were not good soldiers. They also had to get their orders from Britain which was 3,000 miles (4,839 km) away, across the Atlantic Ocean. There were no telephones. Orders from the British government could take weeks or months to reach a commander in America.

Also, the British had to defeat and control all of the United States! It was a huge land with miles of deep forests where the patriots could hide. These patriots were also fighting for their homes and their freedom. They were led by men who were clever and determined, like George Washington. They would not make it easy for the British.

Boston. The American army surrounded Boston after Lexington and Concord. George Washington took command of the army in July of 1775, just after the Battle of Bunker Hill. Washington was a good choice for this job. He was a rich plantation owner from Virginia.

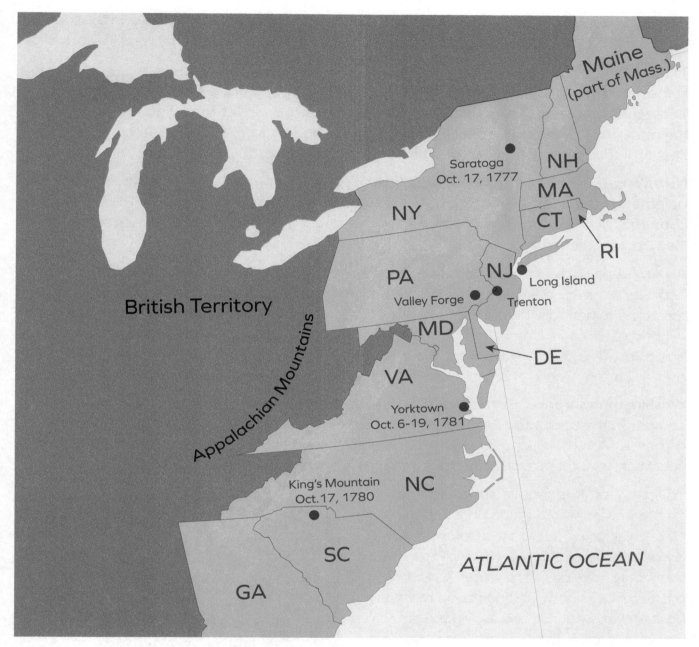

| The United States in 1776, including the major battles of the Revolutionary War.

He had fought in the French and Indian War and the Virginia militia. He was a man that soldiers trusted, and he was a clever fighter. Washington wanted to drive the British out of Boston, but he could not until March of 1776.

A group of patriots called the "Green Mountain Boys," led by Ethan Allen, had captured Fort Ticonderoga on Lake Champlain in 1775. This was an important fort because the British could invade New York from Canada along the lake. (Roads were really bad in America. Traveling along rivers or lakes was much better.) Also, the patriots captured the fort's **cannons**. Henry Knox moved almost 60 of these cannons south by sled during the winter of 1775-76. In the spring, Washington set them up on the hills around Boston. The British realized they were in real danger and left the city.

In the meantime, another American army had captured Montreal, north of Lake Champlain. These men then tried to take Quebec and failed. General Benedict Arnold had been a part of the attack on Quebec. He retreated back to Fort Ticonderoga. In 1776, he defeated a British fleet that tried to retake the fort and the lake.

New York. The British army moved from Boston to New York in July of 1776. Washington was defeated at the Battle of Long Island in August, but he and his army escaped. The British also captured two important American forts near New York City. The British army then settled in New York for the winter.

An American soldier named Nathan Hale offered to get information about the British in New York City. He went over to Long Island dressed in regular clothes. He took careful notes and then tried to get back across the bay to Connecticut. He saw a boat coming that he thought might give him a lift. Unfortunately, one of the men on the boat was a member of Hale's family and a Tory. They captured him and gave him to the British. He was hung as a **spy**. He died bravely saying, "I only regret that I have but one life to lose for my country!"

Washington's surprise. By the end of 1776, the American army was in trouble. They were camped in the cold outside of New York City in New Jersey, and many of the soldiers wanted to go home. Many had signed up to fight only until the end of the year. Unless George Washington could convince them to stay, he would not have an army after December 31st.

In December Washington planned a surprise for the British. After dark on Christmas night, he and the army crossed the Delaware River. It was bitterly cold, and anyone falling in the river could have died. The water was full of chunks of ice that threatened to tip the small boats. With great skill and daring the army was able to cross the river and sneak up on a Hessian camp at Trenton.

| Washington's army crossing the Delaware

Most of the Hessians were sound asleep. They had celebrated all day on Christmas. No one was ready for an attack, but that is what happened. The American army came at them out of the early dawn. It was a complete surprise! In less than an hour, Washington and his men captured a thousand prisoners and many supplies.

The British tried to trap Washington after Trenton; however, Washington was very clever. He had his men leave their campfires burning, and a few men stayed in the camp making noise while the rest of the army snuck away during the night. They attacked and defeated another group of British soldiers a few miles away at Princeton. These two victories encouraged the Americans. Many new men volunteered to fight and the old ones agreed to stay. Some of them would fight for the entire war.

Summer 1777. The next summer went very badly for Washington. The British army in New York marched out and took Philadelphia, which was the capital of the United States at the time. Washington lost two battles trying to stop the British. However, in both battles the Americans fought well, and the army was not captured. The Congress at Philadelphia moved before the British arrived, so they were not captured either. Also, things might have been going badly in Pennsylvania, but they were going very well for the Americans in northern New York.

Write *true* or *false* on the blank.

1.1 _____ British generals were chosen for being good soldiers.

1.2 _____ Britain had a large army and navy.

1.3 _____ The American Congress could not collect taxes.

1.4 _____ It would not be easy for the British to capture all of the United States.

1.5 _____ Tories were patriots who fought for the Americans.

1.6 _____ The Green Mountain boys captured Fort Pitt in 1775.

1.7 _____ Benedict Arnold captured Quebec in 1775.

1.8 _____ Nathan Hale was a patriot who was hung as a spy.

1.9 _____ The British captured the American capital in 1777.

1.10 _____ Washington drove the British out of Boston with cannons taken from Fort Ticonderoga.

1.11 _____ Ethan Allen captured Fort Ticonderoga on Lake Champlain.

1.12 _____ Benedict Arnold kept the British from retaking Lake Champlain in 1776.

1.13 _____ The British army could get its orders quickly and easily.

Answer these questions.

1.14   What happened at the Battle of Trenton? _____

_____

_____

_____

1.15   Why were the victories at Trenton and Princeton so important to the Americans?

_____

_____

_____

1.16   Who said, "I only regret that I have but one life to lose for my country?"

_____

New Hope

British plan. The British came up with a good plan for the summer of 1777. They decided to attack New York from three directions. Three British armies would march to Albany in the middle of New York from the south, north, and west. Then the whole state could be captured. That would separate New England from the rest of the United States, making it difficult for the Americans to keep fighting together. It would have been a great victory, if it had worked.

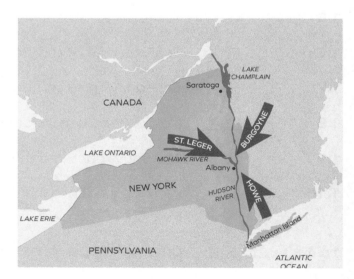

| The British plan to attack New York

General Howe, who was in command in New York City, was supposed to march north. However, he was not sure of his orders, and he took Philadelphia instead. **Colonel** St. Leger came in from the west. However, he stopped when he could not capture Fort Stanwix near the city of Rome, New York. He then turned back when he heard that Washington was sending some soldiers under the command of Benedict Arnold. That meant only the British attack from the north was still going.

Saratoga. The British commander of the army from the north was General John Burgoyne. His men called him "Gentleman Johnny." He liked nice clothes, good food, and parties more than fighting. He insisted on bringing *thirty wagons* full of his own things on his trip through New York.

| Cannons at Fort Ticonderoga

Burgoyne's large army was able to recapture Fort Ticonderoga easily on its way south. How-ever, after Lake Champlain, they had to go through the wilderness. The Americans did everything they could to slow him down. They cut down trees in his path and dammed streams so that they flooded. As he slowly moved south, more and more men joined the American army around him. Finally, they fought two battles at Freedman's Farm in the fall. The British were defeated both times. General Benedict Arnold did a great job for the Americans but was wounded in the leg.

Burgoyne retreated back toward Fort Ticonderoga. However, there was no way he could make it that far. The Americans surrounded him as he tried to rest near Saratoga. He realized it was hopeless and surrendered his army! It was one of the greatest American victories of the war. It was also the *turning point* of the war, the time that things started going better for the Americans.

France. Benjamin Franklin had been an important leader in America for years. He was a printer and inventor from Philadelphia. He had been a **spokesman** for the colonies in Great Britain for many years before 1776. He was sent to the Second Continental Congress by Pennsylvania. He was one of a group of men we call the "Founding Fathers," men who did important work in helping our nation win its freedom and create a new government.

Benjamin Franklin was the American representative in France during the Revolutionary War. He was very popular with the noblemen and their wives there. He had been trying for a long time to get the French to help the Americans as **allies**. He finally succeeded after Saratoga. That victory convinced the French that the Americans would be good allies. They signed a treaty of friendship with the United States early in 1778.

Valley Forge. The wonderful news of the victory at Saratoga brought great joy to Washington in Pennsylvania. He had sent Benedict Arnold to Saratoga with some men because he had to stay and keep an eye on General Howe in Philadelphia. As winter set in, Howe stayed comfortably in the capital. Washington and his army, however, had to camp for the winter in nearby Valley Forge.

| A cabin at Valley Forge

The winter of 1777-78 at Valley Forge was one of the hardest things the American army had to endure during the whole war. They had to build small huts to live in. They did not have enough food, clothes, or shoes. The men were hungry, cold, and sick all winter. Many of them left bloody footprints in the snow from their half frozen, bare feet.

During that awful winter, the patriots had help from Baron von Steuben, a German soldier. All through that winter, he drilled the American soldiers on how to fight. By the spring, the men who lived were much better soldiers because of his training.

The British government was alarmed by news of the alliance between the United States and France. General Howe was ordered to move back to New York after winter ended. Washington tried to stop him. They fought a fierce battle at Monmouth Courthouse, but the British were able to get away safely. The British army moved back to New York City. Washington waited and watched from outside the city for three more long years.

Complete these sentences.

1.17 The British general who came from the north in to attack Albany in 1777 was

_____ .

1.18 The British plan was for General _____ to attack Albany from

the south and Colonel _____ to attack from the west.

1.19 _____ was America's representative in France during

the Revolutionary War.

1.20   Burgoyne surrendered his entire army at _____ .

1.21   General _____ was an American hero at the Battles of

Freedman's Farm.

1.22   The American army survived great suffering in the winter of 1777-78 at

_____ .

1.23   France agreed to become an ally of America after their victory at

_____ .

1.24   General Howe captured the American capital, _____ , in

1777.

1.25   Baron _____ helped train the American army at Valley Forge.

1.26   In 1778 the British army in Philadelphia moved back to _____

and Washington followed them.

American Victory

The West. During the Revolution, the frontier included an area called the Northwest Territory. It was the land north of the Ohio River on the east side of the Mississippi (Ohio, Illinois, Indiana, Michigan, and Wisconsin). There were many American settlers in this area when the war began. The British gave supplies to the Indians and encouraged them to attack the settlers. Something needed to be done to protect these Americans.

George Rogers Clark had an idea. He was a Virginian who had moved to the frontier. He offered to take some men who knew the wilderness and capture the important British

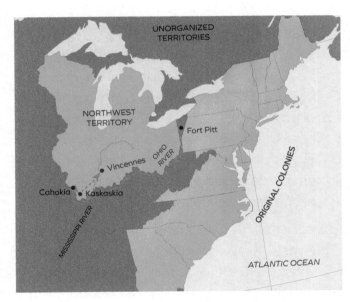

| George Rogers Clark 1778 - 79

forts in Illinois and Indiana. This would stop the British from getting supplies to the Indians. The government of Virginia agreed and made Clark a Lieutenant Colonel in the militia.

Clark took less than 200 men west with him in 1778, but he knew what he was doing. He and his small, determined band of frontiersmen quickly captured the British forts of Kaskaskia, Cahokia, and Vincennes. The British recaptured Vincennes, but Clark would not let them keep it. He led his men through 180 miles of wilderness, including waist deep swamps, in the middle of winter to recapture the fort. This time, it stayed in American hands until the end of the war. The capture of the forts ended much of the Indian trouble, too.

Benedict Arnold. Benedict Arnold of Connecticut had been a great American soldier from the beginning of the war. He helped Ethan Allen capture Fort Ticonderoga, helped in the attempt to invade Canada, defended Lake Champlain in 1776, and was an important reason the Americans won at Freedman's Farm against Burgoyne. However, he was unhappy because he believed he had not been given enough credit for his victories nor **promoted** quickly enough. He also was greedy for money and this led him into a great sin. He **betrayed** his country.

In 1780 Benedict Arnold was in command of West Point, an important American fort in New York. He offered to turn it over to the British for a large amount of money and an officer's job in the British army. However, the man who was carrying messages to the British for Arnold, John André, was captured by the Americans. Arnold fled to the British before he could be arrested. His friends and countrymen were shocked and angered by his actions. Even today when someone is a **traitor** we sometimes call him "another Benedict Arnold."

| Nathanael Green

The South. The British decided to try to take the south after failing in New York. At first, they did very well. They captured Savannah, Georgia in 1779 and Charleston, South Carolina in 1780, capturing 5,000 American soldiers! Using Charleston as a base, the British set up forts all over the state. An American army sent south by Congress to stop them was defeated at Camden in 1780.

Then, things began to change for the better. First, the British were defeated when they tried to take North Carolina at the Battle of King's Mountain in 1780. Second, Congress asked George Washington to name someone to lead an army in the south. He chose Nathanael Greene of Rhode Island. Greene had been raised as a Quaker and had been thrown out of that church when he joined the army (Quakers believe it is wrong to be a soldier). He joined the American army near Boston, after Lexington, and stayed for the rest of the war. Many people believe that only Washington was a better general among the Americans.

Greene realized he could not defeat the British in the south. He decided instead to run them until they quit. He fought battles all around the south in 1780-81. He lost all of them. However, he always killed many of the British and then got away with his army. The British simply could not get rid of him. They chased him and chased him, but he could never be trapped or stopped. The British kept losing men and supplies. They finally had to give up. By the fall of 1781, the British had withdrawn to the cities, and the south was free again.

| Cornwallis surrender at Yorktown

Yorktown. The battle that ended the war was fought in Virginia. British General Cornwallis had a large army in Virginia in 1781. He was ordered to go to the coast so the navy could pick up the army and move it to New York City; so he moved to Yorktown, on Chesapeake Bay, where the Americans and French trapped him.

A large French army under General Rochambeau had come to America to fight with George Washington. A French fleet was also nearby to help them. The French navy blocked off Chesapeake Bay and stopped the British navy from reaching Cornwallis. In the meantime, Washington and Rochambeau left New York City and came south as quickly as they could. They surrounded Cornwallis at Yorktown in the fall of 1781.

The French and American armies laid **siege** to the British camp. The trapped British army finally surrendered in October. They marched out to surrender playing the tune, "The World Turn'd Upside Down." Cornwallis was too proud to surrender in person to the Americans. He pretended he was sick and sent an aide to surrender for him.

This was the last major battle of the Revolutionary War. The government of Britain was tired of fighting. It took two more years, however, for the two sides to agree on terms for ending the war. A treaty of peace was finally signed in Paris in September of 1783 after eight years of war.

Treaty of Paris. The Treaty of Paris gave the United States what it wanted. Britain accepted that it was a free and independent country. America was given all of the land east of the Mississippi River north of Spanish Florida and south of Canada. The new nation was even allowed to continue fishing at the Grand Banks and travel freely on the Mississippi River. In return, the Americans were supposed to try to return the land and goods taken from Tories during the war. Also, any money Americans owed to Britain was still supposed to be paid.

Thus, America won its freedom against great odds after a long, hard war. It was done with the help of the French. We could not have won at Yorktown without them. America would never forget that France had been our true friend in that hour. After the victory, however, there were still many problems. They will be discussed in the next section.

Answer these questions.

1.27 How did Benedict Arnold betray his country? _____

_____

1.28 Who was taking messages from Arnold to the British and what happened to him?

_____

_____

1.29 What did George Rogers Clark do to help the Americans? _____

_____

_____

_____

1.30 What two cities did the British capture in the south in 1779 and 1780?

_____

1.31 How did the Americans win at Yorktown? _____

_____

_____

1.32 How did Nathanael Greene defeat the British in the south? _____

_____

_____

1.33 In the Treaty of Paris, what land did the U.S. receive?

a. _____

What did the Americans promise to do?

b. _____

1.34 Did the British accept American independence? _____

1.35 Who was General Rochambeau? _____

_____

1.36 How long did the Revolutionary War last? _____

Review the material in this section to prepare for the Self Test. The Self Test will check your understanding of this section. Any items you miss on this test will show you what areas you will need to restudy in order to prepare for the unit test.

SELF TEST 1

Match these people (each answer, 3 points).

1.01 _____ Led the Green Mountain Boys to capture Fort Ticonderoga

1.02 _____ He and his army were captured at Saratoga

1.03 _____ Won a brilliant victory at Trenton after crossing the ice-filled Delaware River

1.04 _____ American patriot, hung as a spy, "I only regret that I have but one life to lose for my country."

1.05 _____ Patriot turned traitor

1.06 _____ Captured British forts in the Northwest Territory

1.07 _____ Drilled the American army at Valley Forge

1.08 _____ French general who fought with Washington

1.09 _____ America's representative in France

1.010 _____ British general, lost his army at Yorktown

1.011 _____ American general who freed the south by exhausting the British

1.012 _____ Captured by the Americans while carrying messages between a traitor and the British

a. George Washington

b. Ethan Allen

c. Nathan Hale

d. Benedict Arnold

e. "Gentleman Johnny" Burgoyne

f. Benjamin Franklin

g. Baron von Steuben

h. Nathanael Greene

i. General Rochambeau

j. General Cornwallis

k. George Rogers Clark

l. John André

Name the item or event (each answer, 4 points).

1.013   America's ally in the Revolutionary War _____

1.014   Name the first and last battles of the Revolutionary war:

     a. First _____

     b. Last _____

1.015   The name for Americans loyal to Britain _____

1.016   The cannons used to drive the British out of Boston came from Fort

     _____

1.017   The Americans in New York captured an entire army here after two victories at

     Freedman's Farm _____

1.018   Place of suffering for the American army in the winter of 1777-78

     _____

1.019   German soldiers hired to fight for the British _____

1.020   Congress that became the first government for the United States

     _____

1.021   The capital of the United States during the Revolution _____

1.022   British allies who attacked Americans on the frontier _____

Write *true* or *false* on the blank (each answer, 2 points).

1.023   _____   The British government had more money than the Americans during the war.

1.024   _____   British soldiers could get their orders from Britain quickly and easily during the war.

1.025   _____   The British army captured most of the American Congress when it took the nation's capital in 1777.

1.026   _____   America gained an important ally in Europe after the Battle of Camden.

1.027   _____   The Treaty of Paris gave the United States only the land east of the Appalachian Mountains.

1.028   _____   Americans promised to pay their debts to the British in the Treaty of Paris.

1.029 _____ Nathanael Greene won almost all of his battles in the south.

1.030 _____ The British had a large army and navy to use in the war.

1.031 _____ The new government of the United States had the power to raise taxes only to pay for the war.

1.032 _____ Many of the men in the American army agreed to stay after the victory at Trenton.

✔ **Teacher check:**   Initials _____

Score _____   Date _____

80
/100

2. THE CONSTITUTION

After the Americans won their freedom, they still had many problems to face. The thirteen states still did not work well together. They made a new government that had very little power. It could not solve the problems of the new nation. Finally, some of the Founding Fathers decided the country needed a better government.

Many of the nation's new leaders met in Philadelphia to write a new constitution in 1787. They worked hard and made many compromises. They wrote a document we call the Constitution of the United States. Our government today is still based on that Constitution.

The Founding Fathers also had to convince the nation to vote for the Constitution. Many of them wrote long articles in support of it. Then, after it was accepted, the people had to choose who would be the first leaders to use it. They chose wisely, making George Washington, the hero of the War for Independence, our first president.

Objectives

Review these objectives. When you have completed this section, you should be able to:

2. Describe the government under the Articles of Confederation.
3. Describe the decisions made at the Constitutional Convention and the government created by the Constitution.
4. Explain how the Constitution became the government of America.

Vocabulary

Study these new words. Learning the meanings of these words is a good study habit and will improve your understanding of this LIFEPAC.

bail (bāl). The money left with a court of law in order to free a person from jail until a trial is held.

compromise (kom′ prə mīz). To settle a quarrel or difference of opinion by agreeing that each side will give up part of what it wants.

debate (di′ bāt). A discussion, often public, of reasons for and against something.

delegate (del′ ə git). A person given power or authority to act for others, a representative.

motto (mot′ ō). A sentence, word or phrase written or engraved on some object.

tariff (tar′ if). A duty or tax on a list of imports or exports (goods sold or bought in other countries).

Pronunciation Key: h**a**t, **ā**ge, c**ã**re, f**ä**r; l**e**t, **ē**qual, t**ė**rm; **i**t, **ī**ce; h**o**t, **ō**pen, **ô**rder; **oi**l; **ou**t; c**u**p, p**u̇**t, r**ü**le; **ch**ild; lo**ng**; **th**in; /ŦH/ for **th**en; /zh/ for mea**s**ure; /u/ or /ə/ represents /a/ in **a**bout, /e/ in tak**e**n, /i/ in penc**i**l, /o/ in lem**o**n, and /u/ in circ**u**s.

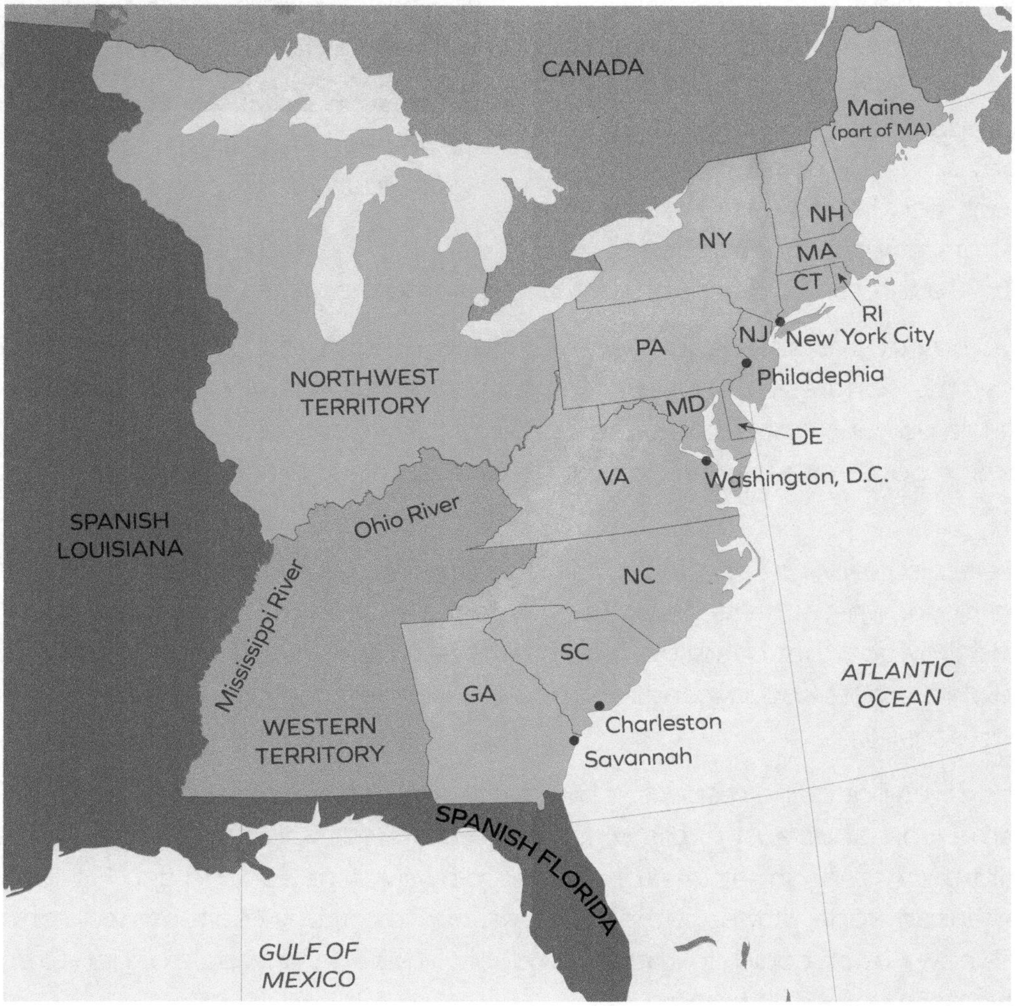

| The United States in 1783

Articles of Confederation

Problems. The Second Continental Congress was the government of the United States for most of the Revolutionary War. In 1781, two years before the war ended, the states finally accepted a constitution written by the Congress to set up a new government. The new constitution was called the *Articles of Confederation*. It was not very good.

| Benjamin Franklin, Thomas Jefferson, and George Washington

The states were fighting for their freedom from Britain and did not want a strong government that might oppress them again, so the government under the Articles was very weak. There was no president to lead the nation like the king had done. The national government also did not have courts to enforce the laws. The new Confederation Congress did not have the many powers it needed. It could not tax, it could only ask the states for money, and it usually did not get what it needed. Also, the Confederation Congress could not control trade or force the states to obey its laws.

The new government was also deeply in debt. The war had cost a lot of money. Since it could not raise taxes, the Congress had just printed money, which was worthless by the end of the war. Without the power to raise taxes, the Confederation Congress had no real way to pay the debt. Foreign governments were not willing to trust the Americans if they did not pay their debts on time.

The states were also very independent under the Articles. Several of the states fought with their neighbors over where the state borders were to be. Many of the states taxed goods like cabbages and firewood that came from other states. Some states had high **tariffs** on goods from Europe while others had low ones. Europeans wondered if they were dealing with one country or thirteen!

The new nation was not being respected by other countries. Britain continued to hold several forts in the American lands east of the Mississippi River. Both Spain and Britain helped the Indians to fight the American settlers to keep them away from Canada and Florida. Britain also restricted American trade with her other colonies. Pirates in the Mediterranean attacked U.S. ships, and the new nation could do nothing about it. Thus, many people began to see a need for a stronger, more powerful government.

Northwest Territory. The new Confederation Congress still managed to pass some good laws. The best ones decided what to do with the Northwest Territory. The states had agreed to give all of the land outside of the thirteen original states to the national (federal) government. The Confederation Congress made some wise decisions about that land.

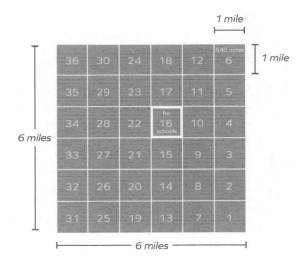

| The Land Ordinance of 1785

The Congress passed two laws, the Land Ordinance of 1785 and the Northwest Ordinance of 1787 to take care of the frontier lands. The Land Ordinance ordered the land divided into townships 6 miles square. The townships were divided into 36 sections, each a mile square. The sections were sold to settlers and the money used to pay off some of the federal debt, except for section number 16. The money from the sale of that section went to build public schools for the settlers.

The Northwest Ordinance made sure that the new settlers would one day be equal partners in the United States. The land was divided into territories that were ruled by the national government at first. Then, when the territory had 60,000 people in it, it could become a state. Each new state would have the same rights as the old ones. Thus, American government and freedom would grow with the country!

Constitutional Convention. Finally, the states agreed that something had to be done to make a better government. They decided to meet together to do that. They sent representatives to the *Constitutional Convention* that met in Philadelphia in 1787. Many of the most famous Founding Fathers were there. George Washington, the leader of the American army, came from Virginia. Benjamin Franklin came from Pennsylvania. New York sent Alexander Hamilton. He had fought in the war and been in the Confederation Congress. He favored a strong federal government and worked hard for that at the Convention. James Madison came from Virginia. He had been a member of the state government and the Confederation Congress. He was a leader at the Convention, and he took careful notes of the **debates** and decisions there. He earned the name "Father of the Constitution" because so many of his ideas were used.

The Convention met at Independence Hall in Philadelphia. They made several important decisions right away. The first was to elect George Washington as the president of the Convention. He was so widely admired and loved that his leadership would be respected by everyone. The second decision the **delegates** made was that they needed to start over with a completely new constitution. The Articles of Confederation simply could not be fixed! Lastly, they decided to work privately, in secret. That way they could discuss issues without having to explain them to anyone from their state who had a question. That made things go more quickly. They settled down to work from May until September.

Put an *X* by the items that were problems under the Articles of Confederation (the ones that are true).

2.1 _____ The president that was too powerful

2.2 _____ Congress could not raise taxes

2.3 _____ States set their own tariffs

2.4 _____ The federal government had no control over the American land outside the original thirteen states

2.5 _____ There were no federal courts

2.6 _____ The federal government was deeply in debt

2.7 _____ States would sometimes tax goods from other states

2.8 _____ There was no constitution

Match these items.

2.9 _____ A territory could become a state when it had 60,000 people

2.10 _____ Delegates met in this building in 1787 to make a new government

2.11 _____ Divided the land in the territories into townships of 36 sections for sale

2.12 _____ Constitution written by the Second Continental Congress

2.13 _____ Met in 1787 and decided to create a whole new government, meeting in private

a. Articles of Confederation

b. Land Ordinance of 1785

c. Northwest Ordinance of 1787

d. Independence Hall

e. Constitutional Convention

Name four delegates to the Constitutional Convention and the state they represented. Circle the one called "The Father of the Constitution."

2.14

a. _____

b. _____

c. _____

d. _____

Write a paper, one full page, about a Founding Father or a Revolutionary War leader. Finish it by the time you finish this LIFEPAC. You can choose someone from this list, or pick another person with your teacher's approval.

2.15

George Washington	John Adams	Thomas Jefferson
Benedict Arnold	Benjamin Franklin	Nathanael Greene
James Madison	Samuel Adams	Patrick Henry
Alexander Hamilton	Horatio Gates	Marquis de Lafayette
George Rogers Clark	John Jay	

Teacher check:

Initials _____ Date _____

Convention Work

Great Compromise. The Virginia delegates had an idea for the new Congress called the *Virginia Plan*. This plan would give every state representatives in Congress based on how many people lived in the state. For example, each state would get one representative for every 10,000 people. This would give the larger states more power in Congress because they would have more votes.

The smaller states did not like that idea. They preferred the *New Jersey Plan*. That plan would allow every state the same number of votes, no matter how many people lived in it. That would mean states that had large populations and paid more taxes would have the same vote as small states with much fewer people. The large states refused to accept that idea.

The two sides fought hard about this. It looked like the Convention would fail. Then, Benjamin Franklin suggested they bring in a pastor to lead them in prayer. The idea was accepted, and after more discussion, a compromise was worked out among the delegates. It was called the *Great Compromise*.

The two sides agreed to the *Connecticut Plan* in the Great Compromise. This plan created two parts for Congress, a Senate and a House of Representatives. Each state would send two representatives to the Senate, but representatives to the House would be based on the number of people. The small states received an equal vote in the Senate while the large states had a larger vote in the House. Laws had to be passed by both parts of Congress. Neither side got exactly what they wanted, but both were willing to accept this compromise.

Slaves. The Convention also had to compromise on slavery. The south would not give up its slaves, and the north had to accept this or not have a nation. The southern states wanted to count their slaves as people to decide how many votes they had in the House of Representatives. However, they did not want the slaves counted for taxes. They agreed to a compromise. African slaves were counted as three-fifths of a person for both taxes and representation. This was called the *Three-Fifths Compromise*.

| Slaves being loaded on-board a ship

Several of the men also wanted to end the brutal slave trade. This was the business of capturing free people in Africa and bringing them to America as slaves. The south would not agree to ending the trade. However, they agreed to let Congress end it in 1808, if they wanted.

New government. The men at the Convention wanted a strong federal government, but one that would not be so powerful it would harm people's freedom. The Constitution divided the government into three parts or branches: *executive, legislative,* and *judicial*. The executive branch is the president, who runs the government and makes sure the laws are obeyed. The legislative branch is the Congress that writes the laws. The judicial branch is the courts, who decide if the laws are allowed by the Constitution and how they will affect ordinary people. Thus, the power of government was divided between the three branches. No one branch held too much power.

The Constitution also gives each of the three branches some power to control the others. For example, Congress can remove the president from office by impeaching him. The president can veto (refuse to sign) a law, and Congress can only make it a law then if two-thirds of the members agree. The president chooses the judges for federal courts, but Congress must approve them. Also, judges can stop a law by saying the Constitution does not allow it. Thus,

HISTORY & GEOGRAPHY 502

LIFEPAC TEST

NAME _____

DATE _____

SCORE _____

HISTORY & GEOGRAPHY 502: LIFEPAC TEST

Complete these sentences (each answer, 3 points).

1. The invention of the _____ made it possible to clean cotton much faster than ever before.

2. The last important battle of the Revolutionary War was at _____ where Washington captured Cornwallis' army.

3. The first ten Amendments to the Constitution protect our freedoms and are called the _____ .

4. The Great Compromise at the Constitutional Convention divided Congress into two parts, the _____ and the House of _____ .

5. America's ally in the Revolutionary War was _____ .

6. The _____ Ordinance said that a territory could become a state once it had 60,000 people.

7. The Americans captured a British army in Upstate New York at _____ _____ after it was defeated at Freedman's Farm.

8. The people who supported the Constitution and, later, became a political party that liked the ideas of Alexander Hamilton were called _____ .

9. The American army suffered from the cold and lack of supplies, but still managed to learn to fight better under Baron von Steuben at _____ .

In this section, choose the answer that is *incorrect* (each answer, 3 points).

10. George Washington _____ .
    a. was the "Father of His Country"
    b. commanded the American army in the Revolutionary War
    c. served four terms as president of the United States
    d. was chosen to lead the Constitutional Convention

11. The Articles of Confederation _____ .
    a. did not have a president
    b. had federal courts
    c. did not allow Congress to tax
    d. did not allow Congress to control trade

12. The branches of government under the Constitution are _____ .

    a. financial   b. executive   c. judicial   d. legislative

13. The North was known for _____ .

    a. manufacturing   b. shipbuilding   c. cotton farming   d. fishing

14. Frontier farmers _____ .

    a. were independent   b. did not trust banks

    c. trusted the Indians   d. had to work hard

15. Nathanael Greene _____ .

    a. drove the British out of the south   b. had been a Quaker

    c. won most of his battles.   d. forced the British to chase him

16. Benedict Arnold _____ .

    a. was arrested and hung as a traitor

    b. tried to give West Point to the British

    c. invaded Canada and defended Lake Champlain for the Americans

    d. fought well for the Americans at Freedman's Farm

17. The National Bank law _____ .

    a. was unconstitutional, many people believed

    b. was signed by George Washington

    c. was supported by Alexander Hamilton

    d. was supported by Thomas Jefferson

18. The Land Ordinance of 1785 _____ .

    a. divided the Northwest Territory into townships 6 miles square

    b. divided townships into 36 sections

    c. used the money from land sales to build roads and support the army

    d. sold section 16 to support public schools

19. The "Founding Fathers" included _____ .

    a. Benjamin Franklin   b. John Burgoyne

    c. Thomas Jefferson   d. James Madison

Answer *true* or *false* (each answer, 2 points).

20. _____ The British had a better army and navy than the Americans during the Revolutionary War.

21. _____ America was given only the land east of the Appalachian Mountains by the British after the Revolutionary War.

22. _____ Slaves were counted as three-fifths of a person under the Constitution.

23. _____ The three branches of government under the Constitution have no control over each other.

24. _____ The cabinet is a group of people that advises Congress and is the highest court in the land.

25. _____ The Constitution does not protect freedom of speech.

26. _____ The American flag has thirteen stripes and as many stars as there are states.

27. _____ America and Britain almost went to war over the XYZ Affair.

28. _____ The Alien and Sedition Acts were bad laws.

29. _____ Southern plantation owners put large amounts of money into factories.

Match these people (each answer, 2 points).

30. _____ Started the first cloth factory in America

31. _____ Inventor, printer, spokesman in France

32. _____ "Father of the Constitution"

33. _____ Second president of the United States

34. _____ 3rd president, 1st Secretary of State

35. _____ Captured key forts in the west

36. _____ Hung as a spy by the British

37. _____ Leader of the Green Mountain Boys, captured Fort Ticonderoga

38. _____ Inventor of the cotton gin and used interchangeable parts to make guns

39. _____ 1st Secretary of the Treasury, wanted a strong federal government

a. Thomas Jefferson

b. John Adams

c. Alexander Hamilton

d. Nathan Hale

e. Eli Whitney

f. Samuel Slater

g. James Madison

h. Benjamin Franklin

i. George Rogers Clark

j. Ethan Allen

the three branches of government check up on each other to make sure no one is harming the rights of the people.

One of the problems with the Articles of Confederation was how difficult they were to change. *All* of the states had to agree to change the Articles. The Convention decided to make it easier to change the new Constitution. Any amendment (addition) to the constitution could be added if two-thirds of the states voted for it. The same was true of the new Constitution itself. The delegates said it would become the new law of the land when two-thirds of the states *ratified* (accepted) it. That meant that nine of the thirteen states had to accept it before it became our Constitution.

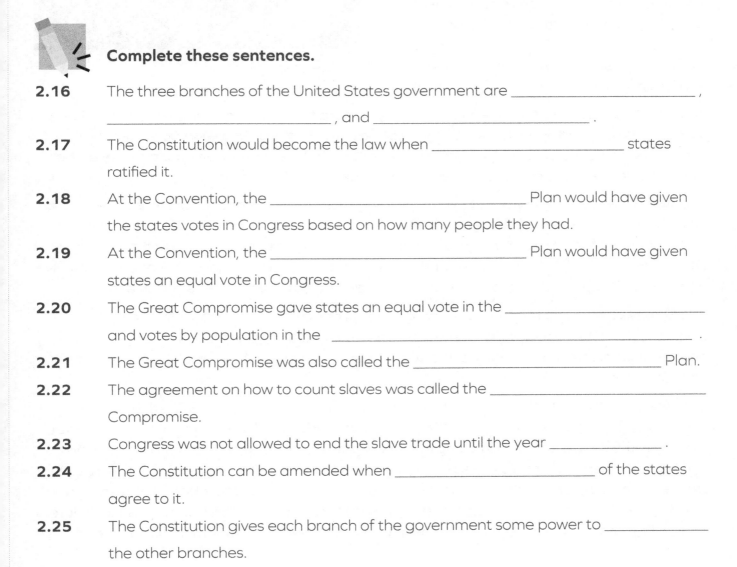

Complete these sentences.

2.16   The three branches of the United States government are _____ , _____ , and _____ .

2.17   The Constitution would become the law when _____ states ratified it.

2.18   At the Convention, the _____ Plan would have given the states votes in Congress based on how many people they had.

2.19   At the Convention, the _____ Plan would have given states an equal vote in Congress.

2.20   The Great Compromise gave states an equal vote in the _____ and votes by population in the _____ .

2.21   The Great Compromise was also called the _____ Plan.

2.22   The agreement on how to count slaves was called the _____ Compromise.

2.23   Congress was not allowed to end the slave trade until the year _____ .

2.24   The Constitution can be amended when _____ of the states agree to it.

2.25   The Constitution gives each branch of the government some power to _____ the other branches.

Ratification

Federalists. The people of the United States had a big decision to make in 1787 and 1788. They had to vote on whether or not to accept the Constitution. People had strong opinions, and the discussions were often angry. Many people were afraid of making the government more powerful. They did not want their state to give so much of its power to the federal government. Other people felt that the federal government had to be strong or the nation would not survive. The people who wanted a strong federal government wanted the new Constitution. They were called the *Federalists*. People who did not want the Constitution were known as *Anti-Federalists*.

| Alexander Hamilton

Alexander Hamilton was a Federalist. He really wanted this new, stronger government. He, James Madison, and John Jay wrote a series of essays that explained and defended the Constitution. The essays were put into a book called *The Federalist*. Many people all over the United States read the essays and decided to support the Constitution.

The Anti-Federalists also wrote papers explaining why they thought the Constitution was a bad idea. They had one very good argument. The Constitution did not promise to protect the rights of the people. Many of the state constitutions promised people the freedom to attend the church they wanted, to say what they believed, to disagree with the government and to receive a fair trial if they were arrested. The Constitution did not have any of these protections.

The Federalists agreed that this was wrong. They promised that the first job of the new Congress would be to make amendments to the Constitution that protected the rights of the people. This promise made many of the Anti-Federalists change their minds and vote for the new Constitution.

Delaware was the first state to ratify the Constitution in December of 1787. Other states followed quickly until the middle of 1788. In June of 1788, New Hampshire became the ninth state to ratify the Constitution, making it the new government of the United States. However, two big states still had not accepted it, Virginia and New York. Without the support of these big states, the new government would not be able to work well. Fortunately, both states ratified the Constitution that summer. The last two states, North Carolina and Rhode Island, ratified it later. Thus, all the states approved the new Constitution, and the new government was to start in 1789.

Answer these questions.

2.26   What were people who wanted the Constitution called? _____

2.27   What was the name of the people who did not want the Constitution?

_____

2.28   Who were the authors of the collection of essays called *The Federalist*?

_____

_____

2.29   What was the first state to ratify the Constitution? _____

2.30   What was the ninth state to ratify it? _____

2.31   a. What was the best argument against the new Constitution?

_____

_____

b. What did the supporters of the Constitution promise to do to correct it?

_____

_____

A New Start

First president. After the Constitution was ratified, the voters had to chose another new government. One of the choices was easy. Everyone knew who would be the first president — George Washington. Washington did not want to be president. He had been away from his home, Mount Vernon in Virginia, for almost all of the Revolutionary War. He did not want to leave again. He did not want power. He liked to live at home and take care of his plantation; however, he knew his country needed him. People would trust the new government more if he was the first president. When the votes were counted, Washington won easily and he accepted.

It was a long journey from Virginia to New York City, which at the time was the nation's capital. Washington was greeted by huge crowds as he traveled. The American people loved him and cheered him on his way north. He was sworn in as the nation's first president in April of 1789. Afterwards, he gave a speech in the new Senate.

Cabinet. America was the only republic in the world in 1789, so George Washington had no examples to follow. He made up many of the customs and rules we use in our government today. One of the first things he did was appoint some wise men to help and advise him. These men were called the president's *cabinet*. Each cabinet member was put in charge of a certain part of the government.

There were four men in Washington's cabinet. Alexander Hamilton was the secretary of the treasury, in charge of taxes and expenses. Thomas Jefferson was the secretary of state, in charge of dealing with foreign countries. Henry Knox (who brought the cannons from Fort Ticonderoga) was the secretary of war, in charge of the army and the navy. Lastly, Edmund Randolph was the attorney general, the chief lawyer for the government. Since that time, all the presidents have had a cabinet to help them, and it has grown bigger. Today, there are fourteen people in the president's cabinet.

Bill of Rights. The new Congress worked to fulfill the Federalist promise to protect the rights of the people. The Congress passed, and two-thirds of the states approved, ten Amendments (additions) to the Constitution. We call these first ten Amendments the *Bill of Rights*. The Bill of Rights protects many of the important freedoms that America fought for in the Revolution.

The First Amendment protects freedom of religion, speech, the press, assembly, and petition. This means you can go to any church you want. It means you can say anything you want about anyone, even someone who is important in the government. Newspapers and TV can report any news they find, even if it is something the government is doing wrong. People can meet together, peacefully, for any reason. Also, Americans can always petition their government about anything.

| The First Amendment protects free speech

The Second and Third Amendments have to do with the militia and the army. The Second Amendment protects the rights of Americans to own guns so that the states would always have a militia. The Third Amendment forbids the government from putting soldiers into people's homes in times of peace. The British did this with the Quartering Act.

Amendments Four through Eight protect the rights of people from the police and the courts. The Fourth Amendment requires a search warrant (an order from a judge) before the police can go into your home. The Fifth Amendment protects the rights of people on trial. The Sixth Amendment promises that someone arrested for a crime will get a fast and fair trial with a jury. The Seventh Amendment gives people the right to a jury when they sue someone in court who has hurt them. The Eighth Amendment forbids fines or **bail** that are too high or "cruel and unusual punishments" (like beatings or torture).

Amendments Nine and Ten are protections against things the writers may have forgotten. The Ninth says that the people may have other rights not listed in the Constitution and those are still protected. The Tenth says that any power not given to the federal government belongs to the states or the people.

Symbols. Countries chose flags and seals as symbols of their nation. Our flag was named the "Stars and Stripes." The Continental Congress voted to make a flag with thirteen stripes of red and white with a blue square in the corner. In that square were thirteen stars. The stars and stripes were symbols of the thirteen states of the new country. Later, when a new state joined the Union, another star and stripe were added. However, people realized that adding more and more stripes would make the flag very crowded, so Congress decided that only stars would be added for new states. The flag would keep the thirteen stripes to remind people of how the nation began.

| The first flag of the United States

The Great Seal of the United States is a symbol that is put on our important papers, buildings, and money. The front of the Great Seal has a bald eagle on it, our national bird. It is holding an olive branch of peace and arrows of war. This shows our country is ready for war or peace. The seal also has our **motto** in Latin: *E Pluribus Unum*, One Out of Many (our one nation was created by many states). The back of the seal shows an unfinished pyramid thirteen blocks tall, showing that the nation would grow. It is watched over by the eye of God.

| Great Seal of the United States

Name the item or person requested.

2.32   The first four members of the president's cabinet:

   a. Secretary of State _____

   b. Secretary of the Treasury _____

   c. Secretary of War _____

   d. Attorney General _____

2.33   The first president of the United States _____

2.34   The first ten Amendments to the Constitution _____

2.35   Number of stripes on the first American flag _____

2.36   The number of stars on the American flag is equal to the number of these

   _____ .

2.37   Bird on the front of the Great Seal _____

2.38   America's motto _____

2.39   Amendment that protects freedom of religion, speech, and the press _____

2.40   City where George Washington was first sworn in as president _____

Review the material in this section to prepare for the Self Test. The Self Test will check your understanding of this section and the previous section. Any items you miss on this test will show you what areas you will need to restudy in order to prepare for the unit test.

SELF TEST 2

Match these people (each answer, 2 points).

2.01 _____ People loyal to Britain during the Revolution

2.02 _____ Decided how slaves would be counted for taxes and votes in Congress

2.03 _____ Where the Constitution was written

2.04 _____ Time of suffering for the American army in the winter of 1777-78

2.05 _____ People who advise and help the president

2.06 _____ The first ten Amendments to the Constitution

2.07 _____ Had no president and Congress could not raise taxes or control trade

2.08 _____ New territories could become states when they had 60,000 people

2.09 _____ People who supported the Constitution

2.010 _____ Congress was divided into the Senate, with equal votes for states, and the House of Representatives, with votes based on population

a. Independence Hall

b. Articles of Confederation

c. Tories

d. Valley Forge

e. Northwest Ordinance

f. Great Compromise

g. Three-fifths Compromise

h. Federalists

i. Cabinet

j. Bill of Rights

Complete these sentences (each answer, 4 points).

2.011 _____ was the first president of the United States.

2.012 The three branches of the government under the Constitution are

_____ , _____ , and _____ .

2.013 The Revolutionary War began at the Battle of _____ .

2.014 The bird on the American seal is an _____ .

2.015 The _____ Amendment protects freedom of religion and speech.

2.016 To add an Amendment to the Constitution of the United States, _____ of the states must agree.

2.017 _____ became an ally with America in the Revolution after the American victory at Saratoga.

2.018 The Treaty of Paris gave the United States all of the land east of the _____ River between Canada and Florida.

Choose the correct person from the list (each answer, 2 points).

George Washington	Benjamin Franklin	Thomas Jefferson	George Rogers Clark
Alexander Hamilton	Baron von Steuben	Nathan Hale	James Madison
Benedict Arnold	Nathanael Greene		

2.019 _____ captured three important forts in the west from the British.

2.020 _____ was a Philadelphia printer and inventor who represented America in France during the Revolution.

2.021 _____ earned the title "Father of the Constitution" for his many ideas and careful notes at the Constitutional Convention.

2.022 _____ said, "I only regret that I have but one life to lose for my country," when he was hung as a spy.

2.023 _____ drilled the American army at Valley Forge.

2.024 _____ was the first secretary of state.

2.025 _____ was the American general who drove the British out of the south while losing all the battles.

2.026 _____ was one of the authors of *The Federalist* and the first secretary of the treasury.

2.027 _____ won the battle of Yorktown.

2.028 _____ American hero at Saratoga who became a traitor.

Write *true* or *false* on the blank (each answer, 2 points).

2.029 _____ The Land Ordinance of 1785 divided the land in the territories into townships of 36 sections for sale to settlers.

2.030 _____ The Constitution gives the three branches of government no control over each other.

2.031 _____ The best argument the Anti-Federalist had against the Constitution was that it did not create federal courts.

2.032 _____ The American flag adds a star and a stripe for every new state that joins the Union.

2.033 _____ The U.S. government was deeply in debt after the Revolution.

2.034 _____ The Articles of Confederation created a strong and lasting federal government.

2.035 _____ Hessians were American allies during the Revolutionary War.

2.036 _____ Americans refused to pay their debts to Britain after the Revolutionary War.

2.037 _____ The states were very independent under the Articles of Confederation.

2.038 _____ America's capital has been both Philadelphia and New York City.

Teacher check:

Score _____

Initials _____

Date _____

80 / 100

3. A NEW REPUBLIC

This section will talk about the new American government, which got off to a great start. George Washington was chosen to be our first president. He made wise choices on what to do and who should help him. These choices helped the new government to be strong and fair.

This section will also discuss what life was like in the new United States. It was mostly a nation of farmers; however, the very first factories had been built in the north. These factories started with new ideas brought from Europe. The invention of the cotton gin made cotton the main crop of the south and made slavery more important there.

Also, Thomas Jefferson and Alexander Hamilton started the nation's first political parties. The new parties, the Democratic-Republicans and the Federalists, both had men run for president after George Washington retired. This set the pattern we still follow today in choosing presidents. The new president faced new and old problems dealing with the war going on in Europe.

Objectives

Review these objectives. When you have completed this section, you should be able to:

5. Describe the problems and actions of the first president of the United States.
6. Describe life in the United States when the new government began.
7. Describe the beginning of political parties and important events under the second president of the United States.

Vocabulary

Study these new words. Learning the meanings of these words is a good study habit and will improve your understanding of this LIFEPAC.

bribe (brīb). A reward for doing something that a person does not want to do.

immigrant (im' ə grənt). A person who comes into a foreign country or region to live.

manufacture (man' yə fak' chər). A making of articles by hand or by machine especially in large quantities.

neutral (nü' trəl). On neither side in a quarrel or war.

term (tėrm). A set period of time that an elected official serves in office.

Pronunciation Key: hat, āge, cãre, fär; let, ēqual, tėrm; it, īce; hot, ōpen, ôrder; oil; out; cup, pu̇t, rüle; child; long; thin; /ŦH/ for then; /zh/ for measure; /u/ or /ə/ represents /a/ in about, /e/ in taken, /i/ in pencil, /o/ in lemon, and /u/ in circus.

Washington as President

President's life. George Washington was an excellent first president for our country. He was very careful and fair about his decisions. He liked proper manners and formal behavior. People came to respect the presidency because they respected and honored him. His many years of service to the nation earned him the title "Father of His Country."

George Washington's wife Martha was a real help to him. She held a party every Friday, called a *reception*, where people could come and meet their president. People were not sure what to call Martha Washington at first. Some wanted to call her "Lady Washington," but that sounded too much like the nobles in Europe. Eventually, people began to call the president's wife, the "First Lady." That is what she is still called today.

Debt, taxes, and the bank. The biggest problem President Washington had to face was the debt from the Revolution; however, his secretary of the treasury, Alexander Hamilton, was a very clever man. He insisted that the government had to pay all of its debt, and he wanted it to pay the debts owed by the states too! Remember, he believed in a strong federal government. He wanted people to see the national government pay off the debts so they would trust and obey it.

Many of the southern states had already paid their debts from the Revolution. They did not want to help pay the northern states' debts too. The southern states agreed, however, when they were offered something in exchange. The Congress had decided to build a new capital for the nation which was called Washington, District of Columbia, or Washington, D.C. The Congress offered to put the new capital in the south. The south accepted. The federal government took the state debts, and the new capital was built on the Potomac River between Maryland and Virginia.

Hamilton had the Congress pass tariffs and taxes on whiskey to raise the money the government needed. He also asked Congress to create a bank for the nation. A national bank could print money for the government and give it a place to hold the tax money it collected. Many people did not like the idea of a national bank. They argued that the Constitution did not say that the government could make one.

President Washington was troubled by this argument. When Congress passed a law creating the bank, he was not sure whether he should sign it or not. He asked two of his cabinet members to write papers on whether the bank was constitutional (allowed by the Constitution). Alexander Hamilton wrote saying the bank was constitutional. He argued that the Constitution did not forbid making a bank and the government needed it to help collect taxes, which the Constitution did allow. Thomas Jefferson wrote the other paper. He wrote that if the Constitution did not say the government could create a bank, then it could not do it.

| George Washington

The president realized that Mr. Jefferson's way would make it difficult for the government to do much. If it could only do things the Constitution said, then very little could be done without constant Amendments. (Imagine if you could only do the things your parents told you to do. They would have to list <u>everything</u> like brush your teeth, play with your friends, and eat your snack. If they forgot to tell you to rest after running, you could not do it!) The Constitution says that Congress has the power to do what is "necessary and proper" to do its job. Hamilton argued that this included many things not specifically listed.

President Washington accepted Mr. Hamilton's side and signed the law. He believed that the government could do many things that were "necessary and proper," but not listed by the Constitution. This was an important thing for the country. If Washington had agreed with Mr. Jefferson, the federal government would have been much weaker. By accepting Mr. Hamilton's side, the president made the government stronger and better able to change to meet the needs of the country.

Second term. Mr. Washington wanted to leave office after his first four-year **term** as president, but his friends convinced him to stay for a second term. The new country still needed his leadership.

During Washington's second term, a war broke out in Europe. France had revolted against its own king in 1789. It was a very bloody and cruel revolt. Many innocent people and nobles were killed, including the king and his family. The new government in France went to war with many of the nations of Europe by 1793. Its enemies were led by Britain.

France wanted America to help in the war. The treaty we had signed with France during the Revolution said we would help them if they went to war. However, that treaty had been signed with the king of France who was no longer there. Washington decided that war would be bad for America. He announced that the United States would be **neutral**. This long war in Europe would cause much trouble for America before it was finished.

Also, during Washington's second term, some farmers in Pennsylvania revolted against the tax on whiskey in 1794. This was called the *Whiskey Rebellion*. Washington called out the militia and stopped the revolt. His firmness convinced Americans that even though they had revolted against Britain because of taxes, they still had to pay taxes to their own government.

Answer these questions.

3.1   Which side did America take in the war in Europe? _____

3.2   What did Hamilton want that Jefferson said was unconstitutional?

_____

3.3   Why was the capital built in the south? _____

_____

3.4   What was the name of the tax revolt in Pennsylvania in 1794?

_____

3.5   What is the title used by the President's wife today? _____

3.6   What is the full name of the American capital?_____

_____

3.7   What was the biggest problem facing Mr. Washington when he first became

president? _____

3.8   What did Mr. Jefferson believe the government could do under the Constitution?

_____

3.9   The federal government made its money by what two ways?

_____

3.10 President Washington agreed that the government could do things that were not

listed by the Constitution because of what words in it? _____

_____

Life in America

North. In the 1790s, more people worked on farms than those who worked at almost all other kinds of work. People made many of the things they needed like tools and clothes. The farmers would sell some of their crops and use the money for things they could not make. These things, like shoes, silverware, and guns, were made by craftsmen or brought over from Europe.

In New England, the soil was rocky and poor. Many of these families had to find other ways to make money. They turned to the sea to do that. As a result, New England became famous for its ships and fishing. The huge forests provided lumber to build ships, and these ships brought in large catches of fish from the Grand Banks. New England also was a center for the whaling industry. Oils and parts from these huge sea animals were used for lamp oil, candles, and making perfume.

| Yarn in a weaving mill

Shipbuilding, fishing, and whaling led to trade with other parts of the world. Many wealthy northern families built their fortunes trading goods from America with those of the West Indies and Europe. Trade also became important in the Middle States. The fine harbors at New York City and Philadelphia were filled with goods from all over the world that the new nation needed. Many of the wealthy men who owned the ships took some of their money to start factories in America.

It was in New England that American **manufacturing** began. The *Industrial Revolution*, the change from handmade to machine-made goods, started about this time. It began in Great Britain where new inventions made it possible to spin thread and weave cloth using machines. The machines were powered by water wheels that turned in fast-moving streams. They made more cloth, faster than people could by hand. Britain protected these machines with strict laws. Plans for the machines and people who knew how to build them were not supposed to leave the country.

However, the Americans found a way to get the plans for the machines. A man named Samuel Slater worked in the cloth factories in Britain. He memorized the plans for the machines and snuck out of the country to America. He built the first American cloth factory in Connecticut in 1791. It would be many years, however, before American factories could make all the cloth Americans needed. Most machine-made cloth and goods still came from Europe because they could make it cheaper and faster than the Americans.

Eli Whitney was another man who was important in helping to start America's industries in the 1790s. He built a factory to make guns for the army using *interchangeable* parts. Before this time, guns had been made one at a time by craftsmen. If a part on a gun broke, someone had to make a new one just for that gun. Eli Whitney realized it would be better if all of the parts were the same in all of the guns. That way, a broken piece could be replaced easily. Also, the parts could be made together in a group so that more guns could be made more quickly! His idea would be used to make tools, farm equipment, machines, and someday, cars!

| Eli Whitney

Frontier. The people of the western frontier were also farmers. They were usually poor farmers. Many of them owned little more than their land and a few animals. They had moved west to have their own land. Their life was very hard. They had to grow or make almost everything they needed or do without it. The nearest town where they could buy or sell things could be weeks away. Roads were just dirt tracks between the trees. Rain or snow would make it impossible to get a wagon through them. Frontiersmen often wore buck-skin (clothes made from deer hides).

Many people on the frontier did not have churches nearby. Pastors, called *circuit riders*, would come around every few months or so. People would wait for a pastor to arrive in order to get married or be baptized. The pastor would hold a service and preach on whatever day he came. Then, he would go to the next place on his circuit (circle).

Western people were strong and independent. They had few neighbors. They were used to hard work and making things for themselves. They often had little or no education. They did not trust governments or banks. They especially did not trust the Indians, with whom they fought constantly.

Put an X by the items that are true.

3.11   The North…

    a. _____ had rich, fertile soil.

    b. _____ began U.S. manufacturing.

    c. _____ was famous for its crops.

    d. _____ was a center for whaling.

    e. _____ more people were farmers.

    f. _____ was famous for its shipbuilding.

    g. _____ was famous for its fishing.

    h. _____ had large plantations.

    i. _____ had no interest in trade.

3.12   Samuel Slater…

    a. _____ built the first cloth factory in America.

    b. _____ paid a company in Britain for the cloth machine plans.

    c. _____ worked in the cloth factories in Britain.

    d. _____ snuck out of Britain to go to America.

    e. _____ had the permission of the British government to go to America.

3.13   Eli Whitney…

    a. _____ started making interchangeable parts in his factory.

    b. _____ made uniforms for the army.

    c. _____ made guns more slowly than craftsmen did by hand.

3.14 People on the frontier…

a. _____ were usually poor.

b. _____ were independent.

c. _____ distrusted Indians.

d. _____ worked hard.

e. _____ could buy what they needed at local stores.

f. _____ only a few were farmers.

g. _____ had many good roads.

h. _____ trusted banks and governments.

i. _____ had circuit riders for pastors.

South. The new cloth machines in Europe needed cotton to make cloth. But, cotton was difficult to get. The balls of cotton had seeds all through them that had to be picked out by hand. This was slow and made the cotton very expensive.

Eli Whitney, before he started making guns, found a way to fix this problem. In 1793 he invented the *cotton gin*, a machine that took the seeds out of the cotton quickly. One person with a cotton gin could clean the same amount of cotton as *fifty* people did by hand!

| The cotton gin

The invention of the cotton gin had a huge effect on the south. The large plantations had a new crop that made the owners a lot of money. Cotton became the main crop of the whole south. However, cotton needed even more hand work than tobacco, so slavery became even more important to the south. Most southern people believed they would lose all their wealth if they did not have slaves. They became more and more determined to keep slavery in the south. In the meantime, most of the northern states ended slavery soon after the Revolution.

Slavery was a cruel thing. The slave trade was part of the *triangle trade* with Africa. Ships carried rum made in America or Britain to Africa where it was traded for slaves. The slaves were brought to the West Indies and traded for molasses (needed to make rum). The molasses (and maybe some slaves) were sold in America or Britain. The rum was then taken back to Africa.

| Slaves at a plantation cotton harvest

The worst part of the trade was the *Middle Passage*, the trip between Africa and the West Indies. This was the part of the trip when the ships carried the people into slavery. Africans captured people from other tribes and sold them to the white traders who came to the coast. These captives were packed into the ships so tightly that they often did not have enough room to lie down. Many died, but enough lived to make the traders very rich. This trade was ended in the United States in 1808, the first year allowed by the Constitution.

Most of the people in the south were also farmers. Some were small farmers who worked enough land to feed their families. However, much of the best land was taken by large plantations, which were growing more and more cotton. The plantation owners were very wealthy men who ordered their clothes and furniture from Europe. As more and more factories were built in the north, the southern farmers started ordering their goods from there, too. However, the south never built many factories of its own. The rich men of the south put their money into more land and more slaves, not factories.

The southern plantations were like little towns. The master had a big, beautiful house facing the river (which was the "road" used to bring goods in and take cotton out). The slaves, who did all the work, lived in small, dirt floor huts out away from the main house. There were barns to store food and cotton. The plantation often had its own blacksmith to make and repair tools as well as a dairy to make cheese and butter.

Life was much easier for plantation owners than for farmers in the north or west. They had slaves to do their work and overseers to make sure the work was done. They had money to buy rich things from Europe, like horses, clothes, dishes, books, and musical instruments. They liked parties and hunting foxes on horseback. Many of them were well-educated. The men were encouraged to serve in the army and the government. However, there were still many small farmers in the south who lived like those in the north and west, working hard to make a living from the land.

Complete these sentences.

3.15 Eli Whitney invented the _____ to clean cotton.

3.16 The triangle trade took _____ to Africa, _____ to the West Indies and _____ to America or Britain.

3.17 Rich southern plantation owners put their money into _____ or _____ , not factories.

3.18 The cotton gin made slavery (more / less) important to the south.

3.19 The worst part of the triangle trade was the _____ Passage when the ships carried the people into slavery.

3.20 Life was _____ for plantation owners than for the farmers of the north and west.

Politics

Political parties. Politics is the work of government or trying to be elected to a government job. A person who wants to be elected is helped by a *political party*. Political parties are groups of people who have the same ideas about how the government should be run. They work to put their own people into office so the government will follow their ideas.

We have a *two-party system* in the United States. There are more than two political parties in the United States, but the two big ones hold most of the offices. Today, our two big political parties are the Democrats and the Republicans. They try to get their people elected in America. These two parties always give American voters a choice. This forces our officials to listen to what the people want and not make them angry. Otherwise, there is always someone from the other party who can be elected next time.

Our country did not start with political parties; in fact, George Washington was elected without one. He did not like political parties and thought they would be bad for the country; however, he could not stop them from happening.

Political parties were created in America because two people and their friends had very different ideas about how the United States should be. Thomas Jefferson believed America should be a nation of farmers, run by the ordinary people with a weak federal government. Alexander Hamilton, however, believed that America should be a nation of factories, run by the wealthy people with a strong federal government. People who agreed with Jefferson called themselves Democratic-Republicans. People who agreed with Hamilton were the same people who had supported the Constitution, the Federalists. These were the first two political parties in America.

New president. George Washington decided not to run for a third term as president. The nation had run well under the new Constitution for eight years. He thought he could safely go home now. He set the custom that the president would only serve two terms (eight years) at the most. Only one president ever broke that custom in all of our history. After he did that, an Amendment was added to the Constitution that limited the president to only serve two terms.

The election of 1796 was the first in which two people were running for president. Thomas Jefferson ran for the Democratic-Republicans. John Adams (Washington's vice president) ran for the Federalists. People still trusted the Federalists who had made the Constitution. They elected John Adams as president. He was the only Federalist ever to become president.

John Adams was also the first president to live in Washington, D.C. The city was designed by Pierre Charles L'Enfant, a French engineer chosen in 1791 by George Washington. The president's house there would soon be known as the "White House." It is a large, white mansion on Pennsylvania Avenue in Washington. It was not finished and was not very comfortable when John Adams moved into it in 1800. In fact, Mrs. Adams used to hang up the family laundry to dry in the unfinished East Room!

| The White House

XYZ Affair. France was angry with America for not helping with the war in Europe. President Adams sent some men to France to talk about it in 1797. The representatives of the French government refused to even talk to the Americans unless the Americans paid them a large **bribe** first.

The Americans refused and went home. They reported to the American people what had happened. They called the French representatives X, Y, and Z, rather than use their names. So, it was called the *XYZ Affair*. Americans were very angry that another nation would treat them like this. The two nations almost went to war. American and French ships fought each other on the ocean. An army was raised and George Washington agreed to lead it.

John Adams, however, knew that America was too weak to go to war with France. He waited until France changed its mind. Finally, the French realized that a war with America would just add to their troubles. They agreed to meet without any bribes.

In 1800 America and France agreed to end the treaty that made them allies during the Revolution. That meant America did not have to go to war in Europe. America remained neutral in that war, but the people in America were still unhappy with John Adams. They believed he should have started a war to defend the honor of the nation.

Alien and Sedition Acts. The Federalist Congress passed some unfair laws while everyone was so angry at France. The laws were called the Alien and Sedition Acts. They made it harder for **immigrants** to become citizens of the United States and easier for the president to send them back to Europe. The laws also made it a crime to speak or write bad things about the government. These laws clearly were unconstitutional. Moreover, they were used *only* against Democratic-Republican writers.

People were angry about the laws and the fact John Adams did not go to war. In 1800 the people voted for Thomas Jefferson, not John Adams, for president. Many other Democratic-Republicans were elected to the Congress as well. Thomas Jefferson became the third president. John Adams had served only one term.

God had been very good to the United States. We had won our freedom from Great Britain, even though it was much stronger than us. We were able to create a new government when our first one did not work well. Our first president made some wise decisions that helped the new government to rule wisely and well. Then, we had two presidents elected from different parties which showed that the officials would have to listen to the people. No one person or group would be able to oppress the American people. They proved that they would fight and work for their freedom.

| Thomas Jefferson, 3rd President of America

Complete these items.

3.21 a. Who was the first president of the United States? _____

b. the 2nd? _____

c. the 3rd? _____

3.22 a. Who led the Democratic-Republican party? _____

b. the Federalist? _____

3.23 Name the political party of George Washington. _____

3.24 France and America almost went to war when the French demanded a bribe before they would talk in the _____ .

3.25 The _____ Acts were unfair laws that made it difficult to become a citizen and punished people for writing bad things about the government.

3.26 Name of the president's home. _____

3.27 What were the two reasons why people were angry with John Adams in 1800?

a. _____

b. _____

3.28 Name the man who designed Washington, D.C. _____

3.29 The United States has a _____ party system.

Before you take this last Self Test, you may want to do one or more of these self checks.

1. _____ Read the objectives. See if you can do them.

2. _____ Restudy the material related to any objectives that you cannot do.

3. _____ Use the **SQ3R** study procedure to review the material:

a. **S**can the sections.

b. **Q**uestion yourself.

c. **R**ead to answer your questions.

d. **R**ecite the answers to yourself.

e. **R**eview areas you did not understand.

4. _____ Review all vocabulary, activities, and Self Tests, writing a correct answer for every wrong answer.

SELF TEST 3

Choose the correct person (each answer, 2 points).

3.01 _____ "Father of the Constitution"

3.02 _____ Inventor, printer, U.S. representative in France

3.03 _____ French general who fought at Yorktown

3.04 _____ Invented the cotton gin and used interchangeable parts for guns

3.05 _____ First secretary of state, 3rd president

3.06 _____ Started the first cloth factory in America

3.07 _____ First vice president, 2nd president

3.08 _____ First secretary of the treasury, leader of the Federalists

3.09 _____ American hero at Saratoga who became a traitor

3.010 _____ First president, "Father of His Country"

a. George Washington

b. Thomas Jefferson

c. John Adams

d. Alexander Hamilton

e. Benedict Arnold

f. Eli Whitney

g. Samuel Slater

h. James Madison

i. Benjamin Franklin

j. Rochambeau

Complete these sentences (each answer, 3 points).

3.011 _____ is the name of the capital of the United States that was built between Virginia and Maryland.

3.012 America and France almost went to war when the French demanded a bribe before they would talk in the _____ Affair.

3.013 George Washington served _____ terms as president.

3.014 The worst part of the triangle trade was the _____ Passage in which slaves were packed into ships to cross the ocean.

3.015 The first battle of the Revolutionary War was at _____ while the last was at _____ .

3.016   The three branches of the U.S. government are _____ ,
_____ , and _____ .

3.017   _____ was famous for shipbuilding, fishing, and whaling.

Choose the correct answer from the list (each answer, 3 points).

Great Compromise	Articles of Confederation	First Amendment
Bill of Rights	Northwest Ordinance	Democratic-Republican
Whiskey Rebellion	Alien and Sedition Acts	Hessians
circuit riders	Valley Forge	Tories

3.018   The _____ said that once a territory had 60,000 people it could become a state.

3.019   The _____ party was led by Thomas Jefferson and wanted America to be a nation of farmers.

3.020   The _____ to the Constitution protects freedom of religion and speech.

3.021   _____ were German soldiers hired to fight for Britain in the Revolutionary War.

3.022   The _____ is the first ten Amendments to the Constitution.

3.023   The pastors on the frontier were often _____ .

3.024   The _____ made a government for the United States that did not have a president and the Congress could not raise taxes.

3.025   The _____ at the Constitutional Convention created a Senate with voting by state and a House of Representatives with voting by population.

3.026   Farmers in Pennsylvania revolted against taxes in the _____ _____ .

3.027   The _____ made it harder for people to become citizens and made it a crime to say bad things about the government.

3.028   The Revolutionary army suffered from hunger and cold at

_____ .

3.029   The Americans who were loyal to Britain during the Revolution were called

_____ .

Put an X by the items that are true for each topic (each letter, 1 point).

3.030   The Constitution of the United States...

a. _____ It was our first constitution.

b. _____ It used the Virginia Plan for making Congress.

c. _____ Slaves were not counted for tax or votes in Congress.

d. _____ The three branches of government have some control over each other.

e. _____ All of the states had to accept it before it became our government.

3.031   The Revolutionary War...

a. _____ George Washington was chosen as commander-in-chief during the last year of war.

b. _____ The Americans won a great victory at the Battle of Long Island.

c. _____ The Americans used cannons from Fort Ticonderoga to force the British to leave Boston.

d. _____ Americans lost the battles at Trenton, Freedman's Field, and Princeton.

e. _____ The British had a better army, but had to get their orders from across the Atlantic Ocean.

3.032   The North...

   a. _____ It was famous for its shipbuilding and whaling.

   b. _____ Very few people were fishermen there.

   c. _____ American manufacturing began there.

   d. _____ Most of the people were farmers.

   e. _____ Farms were usually large plantations.

3.033   The South...

   a. _____ Grew mainly cotton before the cotton gin was invented.

   b. _____ Slavery became less important to the south after the invention of the cotton gin.

   c. _____ Most of the people were farmers.

   d. _____ Rich men in the south put their money in land and slaves, not factories.

   e. _____ Plantation owners had money for better things and education.

✔ **Teacher check:**   Initials _____   **80**

   Score _____   Date _____   **/ 100**

↻ **Before you take the LIFEPAC Test, you may want to do one or more of these self checks.**

1. _____ Read the objectives. See if you can do them.

2. _____ Restudy the material related to any objectives that you cannot do.

3. _____ Use the **SQ3R** study procedure to review the material.

4. _____ Review activities, Self Tests, and LIFEPAC vocabulary words.

5. _____ Restudy areas of weakness indicated by the last Self Test.